THE FOUR SEASONS

JAPANESE HAIKU
WRITTEN BY
BASHO · BUSON
ISSA · SHIKI · AND
MANY OTHERS

TRANSLATION BY
PETER BEILENSON

THE PETER
PAUPER PRESS
MOUNT VERNON · NEW YORK

A NOTE ON JAPANESE HAIKU

THE HAIKU is a seventeen-syllable poetic form that has been written in Japan for three hundred years. It has been enormously popular without becoming banal. For the *haiku* does not make a complete poem in our usual sense; it is a lightly-sketched picture the reader is expected to fill in from his own memories. Often there are two pictures, and the reader is expected to respond with heightened awareness of the mystical relationship between non-related subjects.

This mystical awareness is one of the seekings of Zen Buddhism, and was introduced into *haiku* by the first, best-loved, greatest master of the form, Basho (1644–1694). A second master was Buson (1715–1783), a poet less interested in mystical relationships than in exquisite vignettes. A third was Issa (1763–1827), pathetic, wryly humorous, utterly individual. A fourth was Shiki (1866–1902) — a modern Buson who gives us perfectly-phrased glimpses of everyday scenes and situations.

Almost every *haiku* holds a season key-word; often the name of the season itself, otherwise a seasonal reference easily understood. The reader must take this key-word not as a statement, but as the author's cue to him, so that he can call up in himself his own associations and nostalgias, and read the little poem against this background. The present collection is arranged according to the four seasons — except that it starts with the New Year. Then it quickly turns to the melting of the snow, and the first appearances of Spring. In this book the seasonal key-word is frequently omitted.

Because the poem is tiny does not mean that it is simple. A good *haiku* is apt to be not only subtle but complex, with inner meanings (often because polysyllabic words are made up of syllables which have meanings of their own; often because phrases used have literary and historical associations). Obviously it is impossible to reproduce such complex meanings in seventeen English syllables, and the present translations do not pretend to be literal or complete.

The seventeen syllables of the *haiku* are usually divided into three lines of five, seven and five. Because of the side-decorations in this edition, the longer second line here is usually doubled-up. The reader's pardon is asked for this typographic indulgence. And his attention is directed to three other collections, all the poems being different from these, available from the same publisher under the titles *Japanese Haiku, Cherry Blossoms,* and *Haiku Harvest.*

THE FOUR SEASONS

DECORATIONS
BY MARIAN
MORTON

SPRING

SUCH A FINE FIRST DREAM...
   BUT THEY LAUGHED
   AT ME...THEY SAID
I HAD MADE IT UP
TAKUCHI

EVEN MY PLAIN WIFE...
   EXQUISITE AS VISITORS
ON NEW YEAR'S MORNING
ISO

NEW YEAR GIFT-GIVING...
   AH, BABY AT HER
   BARE BREAST
REACHING TINY HANDS
ISSA

FIRST WIND OF THE YEAR...
   THE OIL-LAMP
   IN THE WASHROOM
SHUDDERS AND IS STILL
OEMARU

6

FELICITATIONS!
    STILL . . . I GUESS
    THIS YEAR TOO
WILL PROVE ONLY SO-SO
                    ISSA

YEAR'S FIRST CART-LOAD . . .
    CUT-OUT PAPER
    FLOWERS DECK
THE EMACIATED HORSE
                    SHIKI

FIRST DREAM OF THE YEAR . . .
    I KEPT IT
    A DARK SECRET . . .
SMILING TO MYSELF
                    SHO-U

SUN-MELTED SNOW . . .
    WITH MY STICK
    I GUIDE THIS GREAT
DANGEROUS RIVER
                    ISSA

7

FROM MY TINY ROOF
   SMOOTH...SOFT...
   STILL-WHITE SNOW
MELTS IN MELODY

ISSA

ICICLES AND WATER
   OLD DIFFERENCES
   DISSOLVED...
DRIP DOWN TOGETHER

TEISHITSU

OLD SNOW IS MELTING...
   NOW THE HUTS
   UNFREEZING TOO
FREE ALL THE CHILDREN

ISSA

A CHILDLESS HOUSEWIFE...
   HOW TENDERLY
   SHE TOUCHES
LITTLE DOLLS FOR SALE

RANSETSU

NOW WILD GEESE RETURN...
  WHAT DRAWS THEM
  CRYING CRYING
ALL THE LONG DARK NIGHT?
        ROKA

POURING FLOODS OF RAIN...
  WON'T MOUNT FUJI
  WASH AWAY
TO A MUDDY LAKE?
        BUSON

CLEAR-COLORED STONES
  ARE VIBRATING IN
  THE BROOK-BED...
OR THE WATER IS
        SOSEKI

IN MY NEW CLOTHING
  I FEEL SO DIFFERENT
  I MUST
LOOK LIKE SOMEONE ELSE
        BASHO

9

OH YOU BAWDY BREEZE . . .
  THATCHER BENDING
  ON THE ROOF
I SEE THE BOTTOM!

ISSA

IMMOBILE FUJI . . .
  ALONE
  UNBLANKETED BY
MILLIONS OF NEW LEAVES

BUSON

SPRING MORNING MARVEL . . .
  LOVELY NAMELESS
  LITTLE HILL
ON A SEA OF MIST

BASHO

PASSING THE DOLL SHOP
  I PICKED UP
  THE LITTLEST ONE . . .
SUDDENLY I SMILED

BAISHITSU

THERE IN THE WATER
COLOR OF THE
WATER MOVES . . .
TRANSLUCENT FISHES

RAIZAN

HAZY PONDED MOON
AND PALE NIGHT SKY
ARE BROKEN . . .
BUNGLING BLACK FROG

BUSON

SILVER-SOFT RIVERSIDE . . .
DIM SPLASH OF
FAR-THROWN NET . . .
FISHING FOR THE MOON?

TAIGI

PAPER-WEIGHTS PROTECT
GAY PICTURE-BOOKS
IN THE SHOP . . .
INQUISITIVE BREEZE

KITO

AH-AH-AH-CHOO! THAT
SPRING CATARRH!...
NOW I'VE LOST SIGHT
OF MY FIRST SKYLARK

YAYU

AN APRIL SHOWER...
SEE THAT THIRSTY
MOUSE LAPPING
RIVER SUMIDA

ISSA

RAINFALL IN APRIL...
TEARS FROM OUR
WEEPING WILLOW...
PETALS FROM OUR PLUM

SHOHA

AH LITTLE WARBLER...
THANKS-DROPPINGS
ON MY PORCH
BECAUSE I LOVE YOU?

BASHO

UNDER MY TREE-ROOF
  SLANTING LINES OF
    APRIL RAIN
SEPARATE TO DROPS
                    BASHO

FARMER, RAISE YOUR HEAD...
  DIRECT THIS STRANGER
    WHO WILL SMILE
AND DISAPPEAR
                    BUSON

GOOD MORNING, SPARROW...
  WRITING ON MY
    CLEAN VERANDA
WITH YOUR DEWY FEET
                    SHIKI

BEACH FISHERMEN GO
    BOBBING OUT...
  BEACH POPPIES STAY
BENDING WITH SEA-BREEZE
                    KYORAI

EVEN THE OCEAN
RISING AND FALLING
ALL DAY...
SIGHING GREEN LIKE TREES
BUSON

I COULD NOT SEE HIM
THAT FLUTTERING
FLY-OFF BIRD...
BUT THE PLUM-PETALS...
SHIKI

GLIDING RIVER BOAT...
RISING SKYLARKS...
RIPPLING SOUNDS
TO OUR RIGHT AND LEFT
RANKO

BIRD-DROPPINGS PATTERN
THE PURPLES AND
THE YELLOWS OF
MY IRIS PETALS
BUSON

14

SHINING ON THE SEA...
 DAZZLING SUNLIGHT
 SHAKING OVER
HILLS OF CHERRY-BLOOM
BUSON

OVER THE LOW HEDGE
 HONEST PLUM
 DISTRIBUTES PETALS
HALF INSIDE...HALF OUT
CHORA

RIVERBANK PLUM-TREE...
 DO YOUR REFLECTED
 BLOSSOMS
REALLY FLOW AWAY?
BUSON

BLUE EVENING SEA...
 FROM SPRING ISLANDS
 NEAR AND FAR
NEW LIGHTS ARE SHINING
SHIKI

THE OLD MESSENGER
   PROFFERING HIS
     PLUM-BRANCH FIRST...
ONLY THEN THE LETTER
         KIKAKU

MIDNIGHT FULL OF STARS...
   DIM CHERRY-PETALS
     FLOATING ON
RICE-PADDY WATERS
         BUSON

OVER MY SHOULDER...
   MY FRIENDS WHO
     FOLLOWED ME WERE LOST
IN CLOUDS OF BLOSSOM
         CHORA

THE SEASHORE TEMPLE...
   INCOMING ROLLERS
     FLOW IN TIME
TO THE HOLY FLUTE
         BUSON

LOW-TIDE MORNING...
  THE WILLOW'S SKIRTS
    ARE TRAILED
IN STINKING MUD
                    BASHO

HERE COMES MR. HORSE...
  QUICK, QUICK, OUT
    OF THE ROADWAY
HAPPY SPARROWLET
                    ISSA

MOONLIGHT STILLNESS
  LIGHTS THE PETALS
    FALLING...FALLING...
ON THE SILENCED LUTE
                    SHIKI

GREEN...GREEN...GREEN...
  WILLOW-LEAF THREADS
    ARE SLIDING
RIVER-RUNNING-WATER
                    ONITSURA

17

CHERRY-PETAL DAYS...
   BIRDS WITH TWO LEGS
   GLITTER NOW
HORSES GLEAM WITH FOUR
ONITSURA

HEAT-WAVELETS RISING...
   PLUM-PETALS
   DRIFTING WAVERING
DOWN ON BURNING ROCKS
SHIKI

COME NOW, PLAY WITH ME...
   FATHERLESS
   MOTHERLESS DEAR
LITTLE SPARROW-CHILD
ISSA

NO BOLD RAIN-CLOUD FOR
   A HUNDRED MILES
   AROUND...DARES
BRAVE THE PEONIES
BUSON

18

IN THE CLEAR FORDING
   PALE FEET OF THE
   SILENT GIRL ...
CLOUDING MAY WATERS
               BUSON

OPENING THIN ARMS ...
   A PINK PEONY
   BIG AS THIS!
SAID MY BITTY GIRL
               ISSA

ULTRA-PINK PEONY ...
   SILVER SIAMESE
   SOFT CAT ...
GOLD-DUST BUTTERFLY ...
               BUSON

ENERGETIC ANT ...
   SILHOUETTED ON
   THE STILL
SNOWFLAKE-PEONY
               BUSON

19

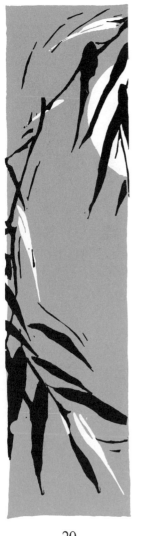

IN THE YARD PLUM-TREES
    BLOSSOM . . . IN
    THE BROTHEL
GIRLS ARE BUYING OBIS
                    BUSON

THAT WHITE PEONY . . .
    LOVER OF THE MOON
    TREMBLING
NOW AT TWILIGHT
                    GYODAI

FACING THE CANDLE
    THE PEONY ALSO
    BURNING . . .
MOTIONLESS AS DEATH
                    KYOROKU

THE FIRST FIREFLY . . .
    BUT HE GOT AWAY
    AND I . . .
AIR IN MY FINGERS

                    ISSA

LISTEN, ALL YOU FLEAS...
  YOU CAN COME ON
    PILGRIMAGE, O K...
BUT THEN, OFF YOU GIT!
                    ISSA

BUT IF I HELD IT...
  COULD I TOUCH THE
    LIGHTNESS OF THIS
FLUTTER-BUTTERFLY?
                    BUSON

HANGING SADLY DOWN
  AMID THE
    MERRY-MAKERS...
GREEN WEEPING WILLOW
                ROKA SHONIN

OUT OF MY WAY PLEASE
  AND LET ME PLANT
    MY BAMBOOS...
OLD BROTHER TOAD

                    CHORA

FOR THAT BRIEF MOMENT
   WHEN THE FIREFLY
   WENT OUT . . . O
THE LONELY DARKNESS
               HOKUSHI

NOW THIS OLD POET
   EMERGES FROM THE
   PURPLE DEPTHS
OF THE CONVOLVULUS
               CHORA

PINIONS PULSATING . . .
   YOUR MIND
   TRAVELING AFAR
BUTTERFLY DREAMER?
               CHIYO-NI

MOON-IN-THE-WATER . . .
   BROKEN-AGAIN . . .
   BROKEN-AGAIN . . .
STILL A SOLID SEAL
               CHOSU

22

NOW HAVING TAKEN
    WARMED WATER...
    THE VASE WELCOMES
MY CAMELLIA
                    ONITSURA

FALLEN NOW TO EARTH
    AFTER DANCING
    JOURNEYINGS...
KITE THAT LOST ITS SOUL
                    KUBONTA

KEEPING COMPANY
    WITH US, PIGEONS
    AND SPARROWS...
LOW-TIDE-LOOKERS ALL
                    ISSA

WHAT, TRAVELING
    IN THE RAIN?...
    BUT WHERE CAN HE
BE WENDING SNAILWARD?
                    ISSA

23

SUMMER

WITH MY NEW CLOTHING
  ALAS ... SPRING
  HAS BEEN BURIED
IN THAT WOODEN CHEST
                    SAIKAKU

HANDS UPON THE GROUND
  OLD ARISTOCRATIC FROG
RECITES HIS POEM
                    SOKAN

AS I PICKED IT UP
    TO CAGE IT ...
    THE FIREFLY
LIT MY FINGER-TIPS
                    TAIGI

FLEEING THE HUNTER
    THE FIREFLY
    TOOK COVER ...
THE EVENING MOON
                    RYOTA

SOFTLY FOLDED FAWN
   SHIVERS, SHAKING OFF
     THE BUTTERFLY...
AND SLEEPS AGAIN

          ISSA

THE HEAVY WAGON
   SHOOK ALL THE
     ROADSIDE...WAKING
A SINGLE BUTTERFLY

          SHOHA

IN THE GOLDEN ROOM
   FRIGHTENED QUICK
     CALLIGRAPHY...
ESCAPING SWALLOW

          BUSON

HE WADES THE RIVER
   CARRYING THE GIRL
     AND SEE...
CARRYING THE MOON

          SHIKI

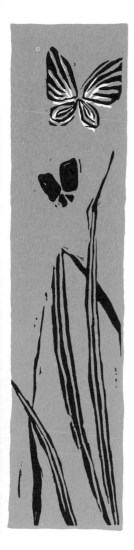

FOR DELICIOUSNESS
   TRY FORDING
   THIS RIVULET...
SANDALS IN ONE HAND
BUSON

ELEGANT SINGER
   WOULD YOU FURTHER
   FAVOR US
WITH A DANCE ... O FROG?
ISSA

BEFORE THE SACRED
   MOUNTAIN SHRINE
   OF KAMIJI...
MY HEAD BENT ITSELF
ISSA

RAINY AFTERNOON ...
   LITTLE DAUGHTER
   YOU WILL NEVER
TEACH THAT CAT TO DANCE
ISSA

26

ON THE LOW-TIDE BEACH
　　EVERYTHING WE STOOP
　　　TO PICK . . .
MOVES IN OUR FINGERS
　　　　　　　CHIYO-NI

FLOWER-PETAL FELL . . .
　　THEN THE ROOSTER
　　　CROWED, AND SEE . . .
ANOTHER PETAL
　　　　　　　BAISHITSU

DARK THE WELL AT DAWN . . .
　　RISING WITH THE
　　　FIRST BUCKET . . .
CAMELLIA-BLOSSOM
　　　　　　　KAKEI

NOW TAKE THIS FLEA:
　　HE SIMPLY CANNOT
　　　JUMP . . . AND
I LOVE HIM FOR IT

　　　　　　　ISSA

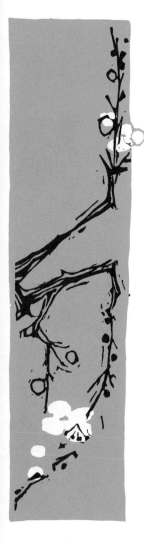

THE FLOATING HERON
   PECKS AT IT
    TILL IT SHATTERS ...
FULL-MOON-ON-WATER
         ZUIRYU

FOR A COMPANION
   ON MY WALKING
    TRIP ... PERHAPS
A LITTLE BUTTERFLY
         SHIKI

AH GOOD BUDDHIST FROG ...
   RISING TO A
    CLEARER LIGHT
BY NON-ATTACHMENT
         JOSO

BATS COME OUT AT DUSK ...
   WOMAN OVER
    THE WAY ... WHY
DO YOU STARE AT ME?
         BUSON

OVERHANGING PINE . . .
  ADDING ITS MITE
    OF NEEDLES
TO THE WATERFALL
          BASHO

SQUADS OF FROGS JUMPED IN
  WHEN THEY HEARD
    THE PLUNK-PLASH
OF A SINGLE FROG
          WAKYU

LITTLE SILVER FISH
  POINTING UPSTREAM
    MOVING DOWNSTREAM
IN CLEAR QUICK WATER
          SOSEKI

LOOK . . . THE PALACE . . .
  YOU CAN GLIMPSE IT
    THROUGH THAT HOLE
IN THE MOSQUITO-FOG
          ISSA

CONGRATULATIONS
   ISSA!...YOU HAVE
    SURVIVED TO FEED
THIS YEAR'S MOSQUITOES

ISSA

IN YOUR SUMMER-ROOM...
   GARDEN AND MOUNTAIN
    GOING TOO
AS WE SLOWLY WALK

BASHO

JUST BEYOND THE SMOKE
   OF OUR SMUDGE
    THIS EVENING...
MOSQUITO-MUSIC

SHIRAO

DO I HEAR VOICES
   FROM FAR LANDS
    ABOVE THE CLOUDS?
O...SILLY SKYLARKS

KYOROKU

SHORTEST SUMMER NIGHT...
   IN EARLY MORNING
   LAMPS STILL
BURNING ON THE BAY
            SHIKI

MOON-IN-THE-WATER
   TURNED A WHITE
   SOMERSAULT...YES
AND WENT FLOATING OFF
            RYOTA

EVEN FLY-SWATTING
   BY THESE BORDER
   GUARDS...O HOW
VICIOUS AND CORRECT
            TAIGI

QUICK-PATTERING RAIN...
   CHANCE AND VANITY
   DICTATE
GAY IMPROMPTU HATS
            OTSUYU

YOU HEAR THAT FAT FROG
   IN THE SEAT OF
   HONOR, SINGING
BASS?...THAT'S THE BOSS
               ISSA

WINDY-WEB SPIDER
   WHAT IS YOUR
   SILENT SPEAKING...
YOUR UNSUNG SONG?
               BASHO

AND EACH MORNING
   RIGHT ABOVE THIS
   LITTLE ROOF...
MY PRIVATE SKYLARK
               JOSO

DON'T WASTE PRECIOUS TIME
   NOW, TAGGING ALONG
   WITH ME...
BROTHER BUTTERFLY
               ISSA

EXPERIMENTING...
   I HUNG THE MOON
   ON VARIOUS
BRANCHES OF THE PINE
                    HOKUSHI

SWAT SOFTLY SOFTLY
   AT THE SICK-ROOM
   FLIES...BECAUSE
I SEEK FOR SLEEP
                    SHIKI

THE DEVOTED CLERK...
   NOT TO WASTE
   A JOT OF BREEZE
NAPS ON A LEDGER PILLOW
                    ISSA

ON HIS GARDEN PATH
   THIS SPARROW
   SCATTERS PEBBLES...
MAN FORGOTTEN
                    SHOHA

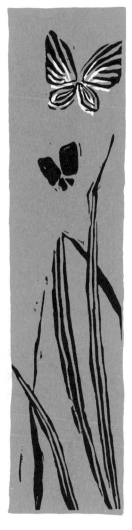

RIVER MOGAMI
   WINDING FROM
      NORTHERN MOUNTAINS
WASHES WARM SUMMER
             SHIKI

SUMMER-NIGHT INSECTS
   FALLING BURNT AND
      DEAD ... UPON
MY POEM'S PAPER
             SHIKI

YOU ARE JUST TOO LATE
   TO HELP ME WITH
      THE LAMP ... MY MOTH
LIGHT-EXTINGUISHER
             ISSA

AGAIN COOLNESS COMES ...
   SILVER UNDERSIDES
      OF LEAVES
EVENING-BREEZE BLOWN
             SHIKI

AFTER THAT ILLNESS
　　MY LONG GAZING
　　　AT ROSES
WEARIED THE EYELIDS
　　　　　　SHIKI

THE NIGHT WAS HOT...
　　STRIPPED TO THE WAIST
　　　THE SNAIL
ENJOYED THE MOONLIGHT
　　　　　　ISSA

MY SUMMER ILLNESS...
　　BUT AT LAST MY LIFE
　　　WAS SPARED
AT THE VERY BONES
　　　　　　SHIKI

CAREFUL, CHAMPION FLEA
　　AND LOOK BEFORE
　　　YOU LEAP...
HERE'S RIVER SUMIDA
　　　　　　ISSA

COMING FROM THE BATH...
  COOL ON HER BREASTS
    THE WARM BREEZE
OF THE VERANDA

                SHIKI

FUI! A SOUR PLUM...
  THIN EYEBROWS
    PINCHED TOGETHER
ON THE LOVELY FACE

                BUSON

HOLY NOON DUET:
  BASSO-SNORING
    PRIEST...DEVOUT
CONTRALTO-CUCKOO

                SHIKI

FARTHER IN THE GROVE
  THE LANTERN WALKS...
    NEARER NEARER
SINGS THE NIGHTINGALE

                SHIKI

WITH THE NEW CLOTHES
   REMEMBER...THE
     CROW STAYS BLACK
AND THE HERON WHITE
            CHORA

I SCOOPED UP THE MOON
   IN MY WATER
     BUCKET...AND
SPILLED IT ON THE GRASS
           RYUHO

MUST YOU COME TO VEX
   MY SICK EYES THAT
     STILL CAN MOVE...
BED-CRISS-CROSSING FLY?
            SHIKI

COOLNESS ON THE BRIDGE...
   MOON, YOU AND I
     ALONE
UNRESIGNED TO SLEEP
           KIKUSHA-NI

IN THE ENDLESS RAIN
   IS IT TURNING
    SUNWARD STILL ...
TRUSTING HOLLYHOCK?
          BASHO

HOT SLOW AFTERNOON ...
   SUDDENLY THE HAND
   HAS STOPPED ...
SLOW-FALLING FAN
          TAIGI

IN SUMMER MOONLIGHT
   THEY GO VISITING
   THE GRAVES ...
SAVORING THE COOL
          ISSA

IN THE MORNING BREEZES
   CLIMBING IN A
   SINGLE LINE
GO SINGING SKYLARKS
          RYOTA

A NEAR NIGHTINGALE ...
   BUT MY HEAD JUST
     COULDN'T FIT
THROUGH THE LATTICES
           YAHA

A SUMMER SHOWER ...
   ALONG ALL THE
    STREET, SERVANTS
SLAPPING SHUT SHUTTERS
           SHIKI

RAINFALL AND THUNDER
   BEATING ON BOARDS
    AND BLOSSOMS ...
INDISCRIMINATE
           SAMPO

RAIN-OBLITERATED ...
   THE RIVER,
    SOME ROOFS,
A BRIDGE WITHOUT A SHORE
           BASHO

39

AUTUMN

IN LANTERN-LIGHT
MY YELLOW
CHRYSANTHEMUMS
LOST ALL THEIR COLOR
BUSON

MORNING-MISTED STREET...
WITH WHITE INK
AN ARTIST BRUSHES
A DREAM OF PEOPLE
BUSON

AT NARA TEMPLE...
FRESH-SCENTED
CHRYSANTHEMUMS
AND ANCIENT IMAGES
BASHO

AN OLD TREE WAS FELLED...
ECHOING, DARK ECHOING
THUNDER IN THE HILLS
MEISETSU

40

THE GREAT FIRE OF KANDA

HEAT-WAVES TO HEAVEN...
   RISING FROM THE
   RUINED HEARTS OF
THREE THOUSAND HOMES
        SHIKI

CHANTING AT THE ALTAR
   OF THE INNER
   SANCTUARY...
A CRICKET PRIEST
        ISSA

SAD TWILIGHT CRICKET...
   YES, I HAVE WASTED
   ONCE AGAIN
THOSE DAYLIGHT HOURS
        RIKEI

A SUDDEN SHOWER...
   TERRIFIED, LOUD
   IDIOT DUCKS
HIGH-TAILING HOME
        KIKAKU

MY MELONS THAT YOU
    STOLE LAST YEAR . . .
    THIS YEAR I PLACE
UPON YOUR GRAVE, MY SON
                    OEMARU

ON THESE RAINY DAYS
    THAT OLD POET
    RYOKAN
WALLOWS IN SELF-PITY
                    RYOKAN

PITIFUL . . . FEARFUL . . .
    THESE POOR SCARECROWS
    LOOK LIKE MEN
IN AUTUMN MOONLIGHT
                    SHIKI

WE STAND STILL TO HEAR
    TINKLE OF FAR
    TEMPLE BELL . . .
WILLOW-LEAVES FALLING
                    BASHO

42

THE EVENING BREEZES ...
   WATER LAPPING
   LIGHTLY ON
THE HERON'S LEG-STICKS
BUSON

THE WET KINGFISHER
   SHAKES HIS FEATHERS
   IN THE LATE
REFLECTED SUNLIGHT
TORI

IN UNENDING RAIN
   THE HOUSE-PENT BOY
   IS FRETTING
WITH HIS BRAND-NEW KITE
SHOHA

THE CALLING BELL
   TRAVELS THE CURLING
   MIST-WAYS ...
AUTUMN MORNING
BASHO

NIGHTLONG IN THE COLD
THAT MONKEY SITS
CONJECTURING
HOW TO CATCH THE MOON
SHIKI

DARK UNENDING NIGHT...
ONCE, OUTSIDE
THE PAPER SCREEN,
A LANTERN PASSING
SHIKI

THEY HAVE GONE...BUT
THEY LIT THE
GARDEN LANTERN
OF THEIR LITTLE HOUSE
SHIKI

ON ONE RIVERBANK
SUNBEAMS SLANTING
DOWN...BUT ON
THE OTHER...RAINDROPS
BUSON

SUPPER IN AUTUMN ...
   FLAT LIGHT THROUGH
   AN OPEN DOOR
FROM A SETTING SUN

          CHORA

SEPTEMBER SUNSHINE ...
   THE HOVERING
   DRAGONFLY'S
SHIMMERING SHADOW

          KARO

DO I DARE DEPEND
   UPON YOU FOR
   FIRM FRIENDSHIP
DEAR MORNING-GLORY?

          BASHO

A WINDBLOWN GRASS ...
   HOVERING MID-AIR
   IN VAIN
AN AUTUMN DRAGONFLY

          BASHO

45

NOW THE OLD SCARECROW
   LOOKS JUST LIKE
   OTHER PEOPLE...
DRENCHING AUTUMN RAIN
SEIBI

HERE IS THE DARK TREE
   DENUDED NOW
   OF LEAFAGE...
BUT A MILLION STARS
SHIKI

UP FROM MY ILLNESS
   I WENT TO THE
   CHRYSANTHEMUMS...
HOW COLD THEY SMELLED!
OTSUJI

WAKING IN THE NIGHT
   I ADDED MY AUTUMN
   COUGHING
TO INSECT VOICES
JOSO

JAGGED CANDLE-FLAME...
THE VERY SHAPE
OF AUTUMN SIFTS
THROUGH THE SHUTTERS
RAIZAN

URGING ON MY HORSE
INTO MIST-BLANKETED
WATER...
RIVER-GURGLE SOUNDS
TAIGI

WHITE CHRYSANTHEMUMS
MAKING ALL ELSE
ABOUT THEM
REFLECTED RICHES
CHORA

PEACEFULNESS...TODAY
FUJIAMA STANDS
ABOVE US
MIST-INVISIBLE
BASHO

SMACK-ACK...SMACK-ACK...
  MEN DRIVING
  FISH-NET STAKES
IN WHITE-FOG MORNING
            BUSON

WHITE AUTUMN MOON...
  BLACK-BRANCH
  SHADOW-PATTERNS
PRINTED ON THE MATS
            KIKAKU

EXQUISITE THE DEWY
  BRAMBLE...
  TO EVERY THORN
A SINGLE DROPLET
            BUSON

FROM THE TEMPLE STEPS
  I LIFT TO THE
  AUTUMN MOON
MY VERITABLE FACE
            BASHO

IN THIS SOLID MIST
   WHAT ARE THOSE
    PEOPLE SHOUTING
BETWEEN BOAT AND HILL?
          KITO

NIGHTS ARE GETTING COLD . . .
   NOT A SINGLE INSECT
   NOW
ATTACKS THE CANDLE
           SHIKI

HIS HAT BLOWN OFF . . .
   HOW PITILESS
   THE PELTING
STORM ON THE SCARECROW
         HAGI-JO

IN MY OWN VILLAGE
   I THINK THERE ARE
    MORE SCARECROWS LEFT
THAN OTHER PEOPLE
         CHASEI

SWALLOWS FLYING SOUTH . . .
   MY HOUSE TOO
   OF STICKS AND PAPER
ONLY A STOPPING-PLACE
             KYORAI

AFTER MOON-VIEWING
   MY COMPANIONABLE
   SHADOW
WALKED ALONG WITH ME
             SODO

AFTER THE WINDSTORM
   FORAGING FOR
   FIREWOOD . . .
THREE FIERCE OLD WOMEN
             BUSON

ROADSIDE BARLEY-STALKS
   TORN BY OUR CLUTCHING
   FINGERS . . .
AS WE SMILED FAREWELL
             BASHO

SUDDENLY CHILL FALL . . .
    WHY SHOULD THAT
    RAGGED FORTUNE-TELLER
LOOK SO SURPRISED?
                            BUSON

ALL THE WORLD IS COLD . . .
    MY FISHING-LINE
    IS TREMBLING
IN THE AUTUMN WIND
                            BUSON

AUTUMN BREEZES SHAKE
    THE SCARLET FLOWERS
    MY POOR CHILD
    COULD NOT WAIT TO PICK
                            ISSA

SEEKING IN MY HUT
    FOR UNLOCKED
    MIDNIGHT TREASURES . . .
A CRICKET BURGLAR
                            ISSA

51

WINTER

LITTLE ORPHAN GIRL . . .
 EATING A LONELY DINNER
IN WINTER TWILIGHT
       SHOHAKU

IN THE WINTRY MOON
 GALES RAGING
  DOWN THE RIVER
HONE THE ROCK-EDGES
        CHORA

THE NEW-LAID GARDEN . . .
 ROCKS SETTLING
  IN HARMONY
IN SOFT WINTER RAIN
        SHADO

WHEN I RAISED MY HEAD . . .
 THERE WAS MY
  RIGID BODY
LYING BITTER COLD
        SEIBI

OVER WINTRY FIELDS
   BOLD SPARROW
   COMPANIES FLY
SCARECROW TO SCARECROW
          SAZANAMI

BATH-TUB FIREWOOD...
   THANKS FOR THIS
   FINAL SERVICE
FAITHFUL OLD SCARECROW
          JOSO

MY VERY BONE-ENDS
   MADE CONTACT WITH
   THE ICY QUILTS
OF DEEP DECEMBER
          BUSON

POOR THIN CRESCENT
   SHIVERING AND
   TWISTED HIGH...
IN THE BITTER DARK
          ISSA

SO LONELY...LOVELY...
   THE EXQUISITE
   PURE-WHITE FAN
OF THE GIRL I LOST
BUSON

IN WINTER MOONLIGHT
   A CLEAR LOOK
   AT MY OLD HUT...
DILAPIDATED
ISSA

BLACK CALLIGRAPHY
   OF GEESE...PALE
   PRINTED FOOTHILLS...
FOR A SEAL, FULL MOON
BUSON

IN MY DARK WINTER
   LYING ILL...
   AT LAST I ASK
HOW FARES MY NEIGHBOR?
BASHO

THE OLD DOG LIES INTENT
    LISTENING...
    DOES HE OVERHEAR
THE BURROWING MOLES?
                    ISSA

A THOUSAND ROOF-TOPS
    A THOUSAND
    MARKET-VOICES...
WINTER-MORNING MIST
                    BUSON

FIRST SNOW LAST NIGHT...
    THERE ACROSS THE
    MORNING BAY
SUDDEN MOUNTAIN-WHITE
                    SHIKI

WHEN THE WATERPOT
    BURST THAT SILENT
    NIGHT WITH COLD...
MY EYES SPLIT OPEN
                    BASHO

WINTER HAVING TOUCHED
THESE FIELDS . . .
THE VERY TOMTITS
PERCH ON THE SCARECROW
KIKAKU

COLD WINTER RAINFALL . . .
MINGLING ALL THEIR
GLEAMING HORNS
OXEN AT THE FENCE
RANKO

SEE THE RED BERRIES . . .
FALLEN LIKE LITTLE
FOOTPRINTS
ON THE GARDEN SNOW
SHIKI

WINTER-EVENING SNOW . . .
THE UNCOMPLETED
BRIDGE IS ALL
AN ARCH OF WHITENESS
BASHO

56

MOONLIT SNOWFIELDS...
   HERE THE BLOODIED
   SAMURAI
CAST THEIR NOBLE LIVES
               KIKAKU

MIDNIGHT WANDERER
   WALKING THROUGH
   THE SNOWY STREET...
ECHOING DOG-BARK
              SHIKI

AS TO ICICLES
   I OFTEN WONDER
   WHY THEY GROW
SOME LONG...SOME SHORT
             ONITSURA

IN WINTER MOONLIGHT
   FISH-NET STAKES
   CAST THEIR SHIFTING
UNEVEN SHADOWS
             SHIRAO

COLDER FAR THAN SNOW...
WINTER MOONLIGHT
ECHOING ON
MY WHITENED HAIR

JOSO

SO CLOSE...SO VAST...
RATTLING WINTER
HAILSTONES ON
MY UMBRELLA-HAT

BASHO

LONG-WALKING LANTERN
DISAPPEARED INTO
SOME HOUSE...
DESOLATE WHITE HILLS

SHIKI

SOLITARY CROW...
COMPANIONING
MY PROGRESS
OVER SNOWY FIELDS

SENNA

58

STARING DELIGHTED
    EVEN AT WALKING
    HORSES
IN NEW MORNING SNOW
                    BASHO

BLINDING WILD SNOW
    BLOWS, WHIRLS AND
    DRIFTS ABOUT ME...
IN THIS WORLD ALONE
                    CHORA

WINTER MOONLIGHT CASTS
    COLD TREE-SHADOWS
    LONG AND STILL...
MY WARM ONE MOVING
                    SHIKI

IN THAT COLD DARKNESS
    MY HORSE STUMBLED
    SUDDENLY
JUST OUTSIDE THE HOUSE
                    BUSON

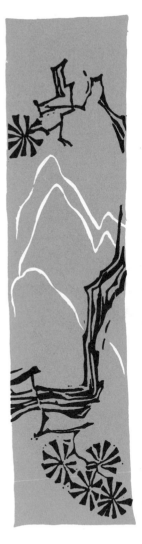

LOOK AT THAT STRAY CAT
SLEEPING ... SNUG
UNDER THE EAVES
IN THE WHISTLING SNOW
TAIGI

IN MY NEW-YEAR HEART
I FEEL NO FURY...
EVEN AT
THESE TRAMPLERS OF SNOW
YAYU

COFFIN AND MOURNERS
PASSED ME WALKING
DOWN THE STREET...
MIDNIGHT AT NEW YEAR'S
SHIKI

TO CELEBRATE NEW YEAR'S
WE FEAST
NEWLY-OPENED EYES ON
SNOWY FUJIAMA
SOKAN

60

DEATH-SONG:

POET NIGHTINGALE...
   WILL I HEAR YOUR
   LATER VERSES
IN THE VALE OF DEATH?
               ANON.

DEATH-SONG:

SUDDENLY YOU LIGHT
   AND AS SUDDENLY
   GO DARK...
FELLOW-FIREFLY
            CHINE-JO

DEATH-SONG:

FULL-MOON AND FLOWERS
   SOLACING MY FORTY-NINE
FOOLISH YEARS OF SONG
             ISSA

DEATH-SONG:

IF THEY ASK FOR ME
   SAY: HE HAD SOME
   BUSINESS
IN ANOTHER WORLD
            SOKAN

61